DWELL

University of Reading
5 Nov 2025

Thank ya so much.

Rebecca & Bob.

by the same author

poetry
ZOOM!
XANADU
KID
BOOK OF MATCHES
THE DEAD SEA POEMS
MOON COUNTRY (with Glyn Maxwell)
CLOUDCUCKOOLAND
KILLING TIME
SELECTED POEMS
TRAVELLING SONGS
THE UNIVERSAL HOME DOCTOR
TYRANNOSAURUS REX VERSUS THE CORDUROY KID
OUT OF THE BLUE
SEEING STARS
PAPER AEROPLANE: SELECTED POEMS
STILL
THE UNACCOMPANIED
SANDETTIE LIGHT VESSEL AUTOMATIC
MAGNETIC FIELD: THE MARSDEN POEMS
TRIBUTE: THREE COMMEMORATIVE POEMS
LX
THE CRYOSPHERE
HANSEL & GRETEL
BLOSSOMISE

translation
SIR GAWAIN AND THE GREEN KNIGHT
THE DEATH OF KING ARTHUR
PEARL
THE OWL AND THE NIGHTINGALE

lyric
NEVER GOOD WITH HORSES: ASSEMBLED LYRICS

drama
ECLIPSE
MISTER HERACLES (after Euripides)
JERUSALEM
HOMER'S ODYSSEY
THE LAST DAYS OF TROY
THE ODYSSEY: MISSING PRESUMED DEAD

prose
ALL POINTS NORTH
LITTLE GREEN MAN
THE WHITE STUFF
GIG
WALKING HOME
WALKING AWAY
A VERTICAL ART: OXFORD LECTURES

DWELL

SIMON ARMITAGE

POET LAUREATE

ILLUSTRATED BY
BETH MUNRO

faber

First published in 2025
by Faber & Faber Ltd
The Bindery, 51 Hatton Garden
London, EC1N 8HN

Typeset by Faber & Faber Ltd
Printed in the United Kingdom by Gomer Press

All rights reserved
Text © Simon Armitage, 2025
Illustrations © Beth Munro, 2025

The right of Simon Armitage to be identified as author of this work
has been asserted in accordance with Section 77 of the Copyright,
Designs and Patents Act 1988

A CIP record for this book
is available from the British Library

ISBN 978–0–571–39447–0

Printed and bound in the UK on FSC® certified paper in line with our continuing
commitment to ethical business practices, sustainability and the environment.
For further information see faber.co.uk/environmental-policy

Our authorised representative in the EU for product safety is
Easy Access System Europe, Mustamäe tee 50, 10621 Tallinn, Estonia
gpsr.requests@easproject.com

4 6 8 10 9 7 5 3

Contents

Welcome Note	ix
Pond	3
Drey	6
Lodge	8
Web	10
Den	12
Hive	17
Roost	19
Sett	20
Insect Hotel	24
Warren	31
Deer Diary	32
Nest Box	35
Hibernaculum	37
Cote	41
Scrape	42
Davidia involucrata	45
Biographies	47

Welcome Note

My grandparents on my dad's side used to tie carrier bags and strips of plastic to the gutter of their house to repel house martins. The birds made a mess of the pavement under their nests, and I don't think their constant chirping and twittering were appreciated either. This was a council house so technically it didn't belong to them, but my grandparents were house-proud in the way of most working people along the row, and bird droppings around the doorstep would have been just as shameful as threadbare washing on the line or dirty curtains. I was ten or eleven when I first saw the bags and streamers fluttering in the wind and don't suppose I thought too much about it; half a century later, I can't help but read the memory as an ironic metaphor. Those birds, weighing less than half a golf ball, would have flown from their overwintering grounds in Africa, arriving back in the UK exhausted from the journey and needing to construct a home. Evidently, the eaves of a jerry-built end-terrace on the side of a northern moor are just as appealing as a picture-book country cottage for a nest site. Unfortunately, at this property on Mount Road, Marsden, they were not welcome and were met with the equivalent of a 'No Vacancies' sign, no matter that a house martin's mud dome clinging to the underside of an overhanging roof is supposed to bring good luck. Over the following decades, this kind of inhospitality has increased in direct proportion to soaring human populations, and the consequence of homelessness for most living things is extinction. House martins are now a red-listed bird.

As a minimum, animals need to eat and they need to breed, and to achieve those things they need the shelter of somewhere to live. To dwell. The particular and occasionally peculiar nature of their dwellings is reflected in the names we have given them: squirrels live in 'dreys', badgers in 'setts', rabbits in 'warrens' and so on. Language testifies to the differing habits of creatures. But human dominance on Planet Earth has proved disastrous for the habitation needs of most non-human populations, even provoking some commentators – with a certain amount of justification – to use the word 'genocide'. It's a tragic situation. Tragic for the plight of animals, of course, but also a pitiful reflection on our own attitudes and activities. Through research and observation, we continue to find that creatures are far more intelligent than has ever been known or believed; increasingly they are recognised as conscious, sentient beings with capabilities and behaviours that are endlessly complex and fascinating. As such, they encourage the expansion of the human mind by example and through the search for understanding. If I describe a planet without other living creatures as 'unthinkable', it is not only because of our interdependence within a highly sophisticated and diverse ecosystem. It is also because I envisage a world where our capacity for wonder, curiosity, invention and empathy would be limited to our own perceptions and experience, a kind of narcissistic echo chamber, one-dimensional in all its dealings. Other living things enhance what it is to be human – why are we so interested in life on other planets when we show such disregard for life on our own?

    These were the kinds of ideas that had been occupying my mind when I was first invited to write a series of poems for the Lost Gardens of Heligan, Europe's largest garden restoration project. After several visits, I started looking beyond the immediate and apparent for something hidden or 'other', a world within its world. The Gardens date back to the mid-eighteenth century and occupy a two-hundred-acre site north-west of the Cornish seaside town of Mevagissey. Developed by several generations of the Tremayne family, they include formal gardens, kitchen gardens, flower gardens, lawns, a melon yard, 'pleasure grounds', meadows and fields, copses, glasshouses, a rare-breeds farm, plantings of exotic and non-native species – notably huge rhododendrons and camellias – and a densely wooded ravine known as 'the Jungle'. During the twentieth century, after many of its workers had failed to return from the Great War, the Gardens became 'lost', or at least completely overtaken by unchecked growth. In the 1990s, Tim Smit and several associates began the long, arduous process of uncovering and restoring the Gardens to something like their original form. They now are a landmark tourist attraction with over 350,000 visitors a year, and a centre of excellence and research in the disciplines of cultivation and horticulture. Protected and carefully managed, the Gardens also provide a haven – both intentionally and inadvertently – for wildlife. Only a small proportion is apparent to the casual observer: the birds that nest or feed there, the more conspicuous insects, fish in the ponds etc. The greater number of species exist beyond earshot and out of sight. This includes some of the scarcer or shyer creatures such as owls or bats, along with thousands of invertebrate and amphibian species, plus some of Britain's largest native wild animals such as badgers, deer, foxes and a recently introduced family of beavers. Many of these creatures are part of an ecosystem that comes to life outside of daylight hours, when the Gardens are closed to the public and offer a fertile, abundant habitat for animals operating under the cover of darkness.

In time, these poems will be manifested physically within the Gardens at site-specific locations and in different guises as installations, noticeboards, treasure trails, recorded readings and sculptures etc. But here they are presented in a book as text, as black shapes against a white background, trying to work their magic and cast their spells. Which seems appropriate given that Heligan itself is a mysterious place, the 'Lost'-ness of its name implying secrets and discovery, something found yet not fully revealed, outside regular space and time. If *Dwell* is about 'the garden' as a sanctuary or refuge, about the locations we must provide and safeguard if we are serious about co-existing with lives other than our own, its simultaneous meaning is as an encouragement to slow down and spend time with ideas. 'Don't dwell on it,' people say, but I'm saying, 'Please do.' And the poems themselves are dwellings, too – constructions built from language and contemplation, places to enter.

Come in, you are welcome.

SIMON ARMITAGE, 2025

DWELL

Pond

If a pine cone
or seed propeller
splashes down

on the glassy water's
two-way mirror,
the spell is broken.

But the skin mends —
the troubled surface
glazes over, resets

and forms a film
starring newts
and swallows.

Drey

It's a twig-and-leaf crow's-nest squat
wombed with feathers and moss
wedged in the fork of an oak.

At dawn she marches head first
down the slippery trunk, back feet
swivelled south-to-north,
then takes stock on the ground,
freezes when the world twitches,
fidgets and jerks when the world holds still.
She's wearing her soft work-gloves
to tackle today's jobs:
a smash-and-grab raid on a garden feeder,
planting the future,
trapezing from spindly birch to spidery beech
over a thundering stream,
bringing herself home.
It's a non-stop stop-motion life,
her brain always in scavenge-and-forage mode,
the universe cupped
in the bright black bead of her eye.
In spring sunlight
under the flare of noon she sploots

on a flat stone to cool off
then rockets about in knotted undergrowth.

All day her tail
balanced and mimicked her every move.
At dusk, as a silhouette on the bough of a maple,
that tail is a question mark
and the answer is squirrel.

Lodge

Like a cabin without a door,
a kindling hut
that's all roof and no windows,

a rickety logjam
rafting in midstream,
a flat-pack chalet

dropped from a great height
then cobbled together
with sludge and stones.

For all we know,
the beavers inside are watching
cable TV,

reading *House and Garden*
in velour lounge-wear
and sipping Earl Grey.

For all we know,
the interior decor might be High Gothic
or shabby chic.

But outside
it's a spillikin stave church,
a scuppered galleon hull

run aground,
a drowned bonfire or washed-up woodpile,
a lumberyard after a force 10 gale,

strewn timber like sharpened pencils
felled by iron teeth, teeth
that have grown bodies and tails.

Web

Abseiling silk threads,
spiders darn holes in the hedge.
Trampolines of death.

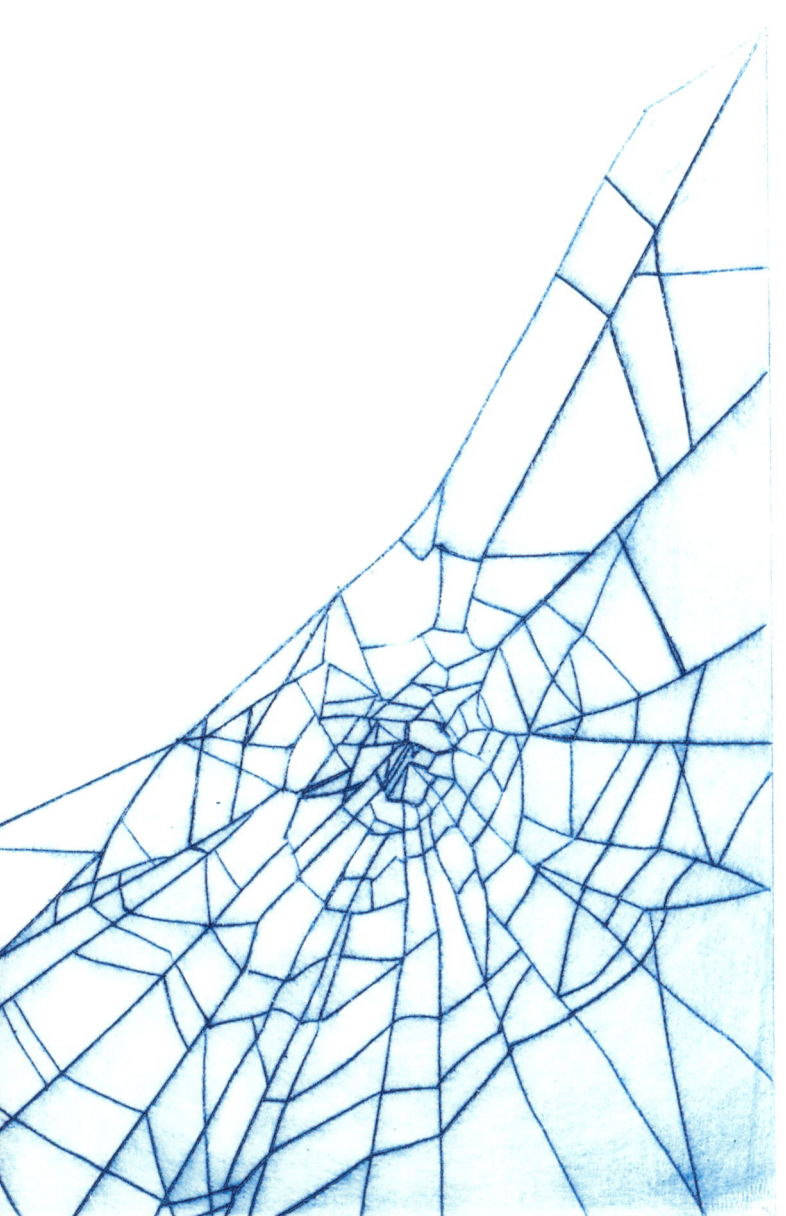

Den

For the pelt, harvest bushels
of dead bracken
quickened with poppy blood.

Coax forked lightning
onto a barbed wire fence to forge the teeth.
The incisors are quartz, the claws flint.

The tail is a copper beech hedge
backcombed by west winds
and tipped with snow.

The reflection of Sirius
balanced in two puddles of fresh rain
will serve as the eyes.

For the tongue,
bury raw meat for a month
till the maggots dance.

Then, from daylight's cauldron,
pour everything earthwards
flooding the chambers and lairs

and seal the kiln
with the door of night.
Into a wet morning,

out of ash and filth a fox emerges
dripping with flames,
setting the mind on fire.

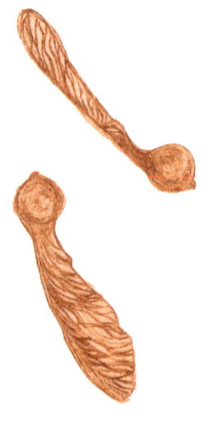

Hive

The weather inside
is always a blazing storm,

feverish cells colliding,
particles being drawn in,

bashed around, thrown out.
Imagine dipping your hand

into the swarm,
feeling the furious blizzard

at the reactor's core.
Imagine the same frenzy

of fusion and fission
conjuring up

the wrought hexagonal what-the-heck
of a honeycomb

and jars of sunlight
in edible form.

Roost

The sun fizzles out.
Bats unhug themselves and fly –
they will eat the night.

Sett

Imagine a badger moving past human things,
crossing the stream on stepping stones
then climbing the steps to the gravel path,
the treads and risers exactly the wrong gauge
for its low-slung frame and footstool legs.
And then on the groomed lawn by the big house
pronging the soil for grubs, its hippy coat
silvered by porch lights and carriage lamps.
It passes the bee boles without looking up,
rounds the fluted plinth of a sundial
telling the wrong time under a fat moon.
Imagine it standing up like a toddler to lap
from the bird bath, clocking its own burglar's face
in the French windows, think of it shuffling along
through the melon yard where beaver-tailed glass
distils dew into cast iron gutters and butts,
notice its long snout hoovering smells
by the bins, stare at its sticky tongue
blotting woodlice, earwigs and snails
from the compost heap and summerhouse floor.
Picture its shaving-brush rump dusting the farm gate.
In the walled garden its shadow scuttles
brick to brick, then it scrabbles and fossicks
below the elephant ears in the rhubarb patch.

With the night shift over it goes to ground
in blind tunnels hung with wiry roots
under roads, parks, floorboards and footings,
stashes itself in deep starless holes with its clan.
In the warm dark the cubs rise like loaves.

Insect Hotel

'We were somewhat distressed by the cockroaches in our bedroom, until we remembered we ARE cockroaches, then felt very at home.'

'Sketchy phone signal and rubbish Wi-Fi. I'm all for being green and environmentally righteous etc. etc. but not if it means living in the dark ages.'

'Stopped here overnight on the way to a decaying oak a couple of miles away and ended up hibernating for the whole winter. Would deffo recommend. Dreamland!'

'Thin walls, earwigs next door, felt very overheard.'

'Dark and dingy. Had to ask a glow-worm to show me to my room.'

'Just checking out when – whoooaaa, natterjack toad INCOMING. NATTERJACK TOAD, swoon. Absolute gentleman, got a selfie, can die happy now.'

'Room too small but great buffet breakfast. Fresh baby woodlice the best I've tasted.'

'Lift doesn't work. Got stuck behind an old snail on the stairs. I was like, get a wriggle on, granddad. Call me snailist but why stay at a hotel when you've got your own house on your back, right?'

'A little bit off the beaten track but decent nightlife.'

'Creepy.'

'Lousy.'

'As a dormouse, I was slightly surprised to be sharing a room with a hedgehog, thought he might be a bit of a prickly character (lol winking face emoji), but we rubbed along (ouch! lol winking face emoji) very well and have kept in touch (ouch again! lol winking face emoji) ever since (smiley face emoji)'

'To whom it may concern, the bar was full of inebriated bees – I think there had been a big match, they were extremely intoxicated, downing nectar like there was no tomorrow, dressed in team colours. Wolverhampton Wanderers? Wasps? Mrs Lacewing and myself found them very intimidating. Haven't they got hives to go to?'

'Amazing Beetles tribute band in the function room.'

'I am not a stick – I am a *stick insect* – so it's VERY annoying to have a snooze in the bar only to wake up and find that someone has "tidied me away" in the umbrella-stand or is using me to help them hobble around the gardens. Also, NB, FYI, I am not a snooker cue. Would you be happy if you came round from an afternoon nap to discover someone whittling your leg into a Welsh love spoon?'

'Left my shoes outside my room and in the morning they'd been properly cleaned and polished. Thank you a hundred times over. You made this centipede very happy.'

'Horrendous. Brought the kids with us but next morning they'd been eaten by a dunnock. No refund or apology, not even a drinks voucher. Two thumbs down.'

'Booked a standard fallen log but got upgraded to junior birch-bark suite with a view of Mevagissey. Result!'

'No parking.'

'Great buzz.'

'Thought we'd walked in on a *Dr Who* or *Star Trek* convention but it was a ladybird conference, the place crawling with 'em.'

'Mouldy and damp. Mice. Cobwebs everywhere. Perfect.'

Warren

Rabbits lurk and skulk
in the brain of the burrow.
The hill is thinking.

Deer Diary

MONDAY
A grey deer?
No, wood smoke drifting from a poacher's fire.

TUESDAY
A brown fawn?
No, a heap of autumn leaves ruffled by wind.

WEDNESDAY
A black stag?
No, the cosmic darkness between trees.

THURSDAY
A white hart?
No, the first snow of winter, very late.

FRIDAY
A red doe?
No, dusk stubbing out its last cigar of the day.

SATURDAY
A golden hind?
No, just heat haze in the barley field.

SUNDAY
A silver birch lancing a full moon?
No, a unicorn.

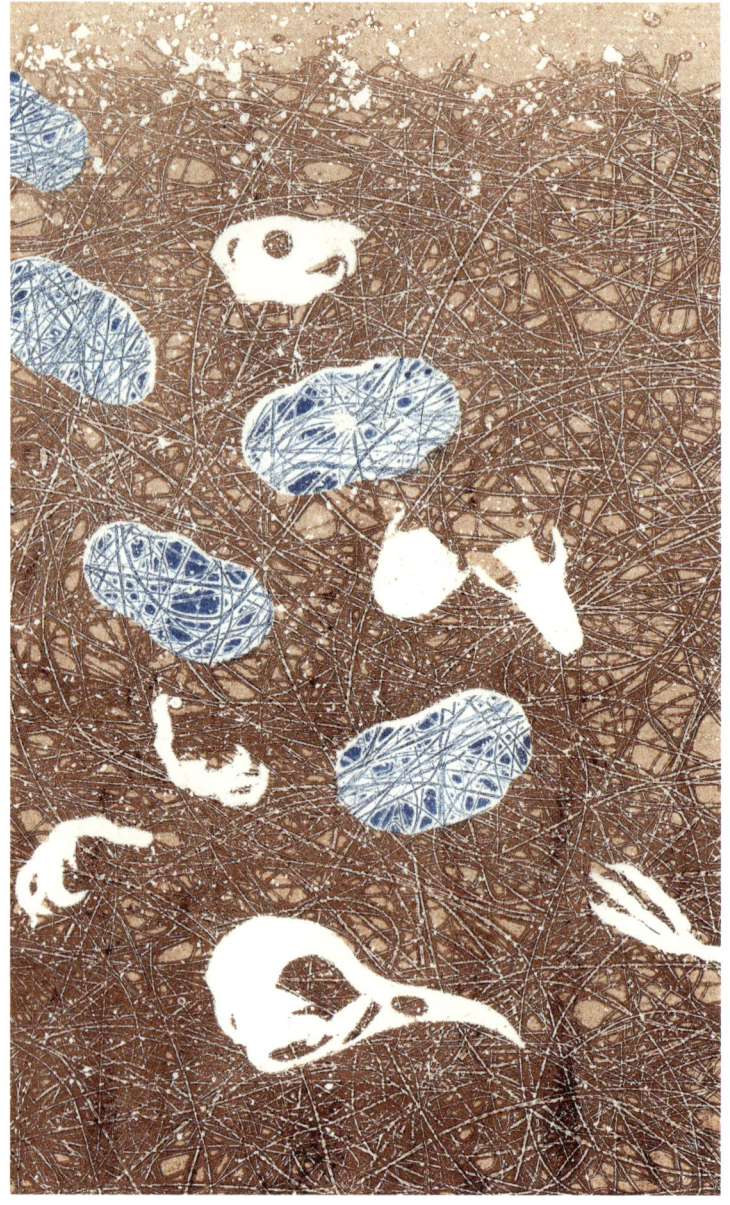

Nest Box

When the drunken old fool
saw the barn owl,

he swore blind it was an angel.
'Half-human, half-eagle,'

he told someone in the town square.
'White flames in mid-air,

a ghost with wings,' he crowed
to the gathering crowd.

'A weird presence
that materialised out of the heavens,'

he said to the scrum of reporters
before he keeled over.

They searched the meadow and heath
but found only pellets of small bones and teeth

and skulls and part-digested fur
and knotted hair.

Which was strange, because when the young girl
saw the angel she swore blind it was a barn owl,

but when birdwatchers went to the copse
and looked in the nest box

they found tinselly silver threads
and luminous turds

and a warm meteorite
and a few feathers made only of light.

Hibernaculum

Spiky boxing gloves,
hedgehogs curl up below ground.
Winter shakes its fist.

Cote

a song without a tune

So please don't make me rhyme with love.
It's hard enough anyway being the bird
of hope and peace; I can't be the dove
of hearts as well. I'm not that word.

I'm a single soul in a sexy hotel
so please don't make me rhyme with love;
the jackdaws want me to go to hell,
and when it comes to push and shove

they've got the beaks and claws to prove
a point. A clattering is what they are.
So please don't make me rhyme with love;
that really would be a flight too far

for a creature made of sugar and sleet,
on a wing and a prayer. And, heavens above,
I'm on my own in the honeymoon suite,
so please don't make me rhyme with love.

Scrape

They say every hare
is a broken heart
with legs, hatched
from the moon's egg.

In a dint in the earth
with its ears flattened
and its body no more
than a poured puddle

of brown fur,
this one lies low
till a boot or dog or tyre
comes within inches.

Then, once triggered,
it springs up, shape-shifts
into an awkward contraption
and hurtles towards the void.

At which moment,
somewhere out in the world,
Love falls asleep with its eyes open
and a door closes.

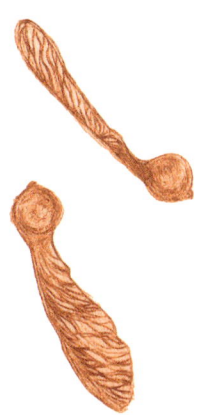

Davidia involucrata

Say hello to spring.
White handkerchiefs are waving
to bring home the bees.

*

Summer's siege begins.
Waving white handkerchiefs, May
surrenders to June.

*

By late September,
yellow leaves don't remember
the white handkerchiefs.

*

Winter waves its wand.
Ta-dah – pocket handkerchief
becomes candyfloss.

Simon Armitage was born in West Yorkshire and is Professor of Poetry at the University of Leeds. His collections of poetry, which have received numerous prizes and awards, include *Seeing Stars* (2010), *The Unaccompanied* (2017), *Sandettie Light Vessel Automatic* (2019), *Magnetic Field* (2020), *Blossomise* (2024) and his acclaimed translation of *Sir Gawain and the Green Knight* (2007). He writes extensively for television and radio, and is the author of two novels and the non-fiction bestsellers *All Points North* (1998), *Walking Home* (2012) and *Walking Away* (2015). His theatre works include *The Last Days of Troy*, performed at Shakespeare's Globe in 2014. From 2015 to 2019, he served as Professor of Poetry at the University of Oxford, and, in 2018, he was awarded the Queen's Gold Medal for Poetry. Simon Armitage is Poet Laureate.

Beth Munro is a hybrid printmaker and illustrator living in South East Cornwall. She loves to explore combining different printmaking techniques to create original work that celebrates the natural world, be it land or sea.